JUST LOOK AT...

LIVING AT THE POLES

Bernard Stonehouse

Macdonald Educational

Factual Advisor: Dr. Christopher Green

Editor: Peter Harrison
Teacher Panel: John Allen, Lynn McCoombe,
Ann Merriman
Designer: Ewing Paddock
Production: Rosemary Bishop
Picture Research: Kathy Lockley

Illustrations
Ashley Boon/M. Mundy 16–17, 20–21
John Booth/M. Mundy 8–9, 10–11, 12–13
Lorraine Calaora/M. Mundy Cover cartoon, 9, 16,
22, 22–23, 32, 36
Andrew Pagram/M. Mundy 14–15, 18–19,
28–29, 36–37
Raymond Turvey 24, 33, 34, 35, 40

Photographs
Bryan & Cherry Alexander, cover,
18–19, 23, 28–29, 30, 30–31, 31
Arctic Camera/Derek Fordham, 10–11, 17
British Antarctic Survey/C.J. Gilbert, 38, 43/
B. Herrod, 41 /J. Loynes, 39
Douglas Botting, 25
British Library, 20
Bruce Coleman Ltd./Jen & Les Bartlett, 8, 36 /
I. Iverson, 37
Robert Harding Picture Library, title page, 13, 15,
24–25, 40–41
Michael Holford, 32–33T
Royal Geographical Society, 34–35
Scott Polar Research Institute, 42
Bernard Stonehouse, 32–33B
Tass, 26–27
ZEFA, 26, 27

Title page photo.: Part of the town of
Angmagssalik, capital of Greenland

British Library Cataloguing in Publication Data
Stonehouse, Bernard
    Living at the Poles.—(Just look at)
    1. Polar Regions—Social life and customs—
    Juvenile literature
    I. Title   II. Series
    910'.0911   G590

ISBN 0-356-11187-3

How to use this book
Look first in the contents page to see if the subject you want is listed. For instance, if you want to find out about the Inuit, you will find the information on pages 30 and 31. The word list explains the more difficult terms found in this book. The index will tell you how many times a particular subject is mentioned and whether there is a picture of it.

Living at the Poles is one of a series of books on how people live. All the books on this subject have an orange colour band around the cover. If you want to know more about how people live, look for other books with an orange colour band in the **Just Look At . . .** series.

A MACDONALD BOOK
© Macdonald & Co. (Publishers) Ltd. 1986

First published in Great Britain in 1986
by Macdonald & Co. (Publishers) Ltd.
London & Sydney.

Printed and bound in Great Britain by Purnell & Sons
(Book Production) Ltd. Paulton, nr. Bristol.

Macdonald & Co. (Publishers) Ltd.
Greater London House, Hampstead Road, London NW1 7QX

CONTENTS

WHERE ARE THE POLES?

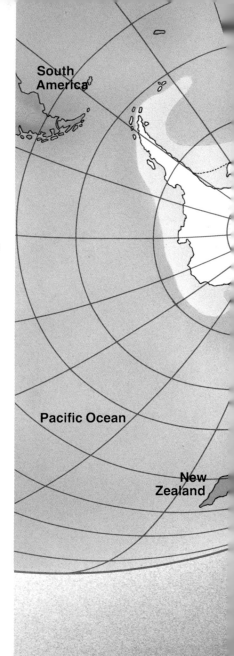

South
America

Pacific Ocean

New
Zealand

Our world is a huge ball or sphere 12,756 kilometres in diameter. If you spin an ordinary ball, you'll see that one point on the top doesn't seem to move. There is another point at the bottom just like it. These points are called poles of rotation. The Earth spins, just like a ball, once every 24 hours. The Earth's poles of rotation are called the North and South Poles. Maps of the world usually show the North Pole and the region around it at the top, and the south polar region at the bottom. Special polar maps, like the ones here and on the next few pages, show one polar region at a time, with the Pole itself in the middle.

The polar regions are cold, icy deserts. During its winter the southern polar (antarctic) region is the coldest place on Earth, and it is bitterly cold even at the height of its summer. The north polar (arctic) region is not quite so cold but is still icy all year round, and much colder than most people like for living in. Very few people live at either end of the world, and those who do have to find special ways of living and coping with the constant cold.

There is no day and night; instead there are five or six months of darkness in winter, followed by five or six months of summer daylight. There is no east and west; at the South Pole every direction is north, and at the North Pole every direction you go in is south.

Tundra coastline in spring, Hudson Bay, Canada. This aerial photograph shows tundra in the foreground, still partly covered with snow and melt-pools. In the middle distance, sea ice is starting to break up, but it is still completely frozen farther out towards the sea. ▶

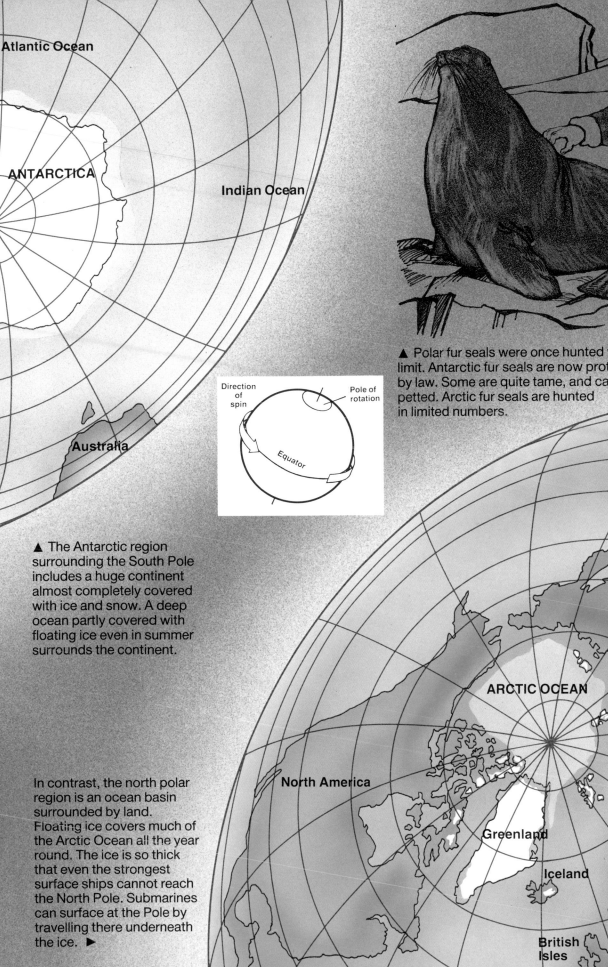

Atlantic Ocean

ANTARCTICA

Indian Ocean

Australia

Direction of spin
Pole of rotation
Equator

▲ Polar fur seals were once hunted without limit. Antarctic fur seals are now protected by law. Some are quite tame, and can be petted. Arctic fur seals are hunted in limited numbers.

▲ The Antarctic region surrounding the South Pole includes a huge continent almost completely covered with ice and snow. A deep ocean partly covered with floating ice even in summer surrounds the continent.

In contrast, the north polar region is an ocean basin surrounded by land. Floating ice covers much of the Arctic Ocean all the year round. The ice is so thick that even the strongest surface ships cannot reach the North Pole. Submarines can surface at the Pole by travelling there underneath the ice. ▶

USSR

ARCTIC OCEAN

North America

Greenland

Iceland

British Isles

Europe

Around the North Pole

If you are at the North Pole, you will be standing on a floe of ice and snow perhaps as big as a football field. The ice will be two or three metres thick, with other floes stretching away to the horizon in all directions. The ice floats on the deep Arctic Ocean, and the nearest land, Cape Morris Jesup, is 700 kilometres away on the northern shore of Greenland.

You may have walked to the Pole over the sea ice with skis and dog teams, like the first men who reached the North Pole earlier this century. You could have landed by aircraft or from a submarine, or come part of the way by icebreaker. You might even have drifted there, because the sea ice itself is constantly shifting.

How to survive
If you are staying any length of time you will need a strong tent or a hut, well insulated against the cold and anchored securely to the ice to prevent the wind carrying it away. If it is summer the Sun will probably be shining, but you'll need plenty of warm clothing, because temperatures can fall as low as −30 °C, even in the Sun. You'll need a stove to keep you warm, fuel to run it, and food, because there is nothing outside to eat, and the nearest store is 1000 kilometres away across the ice in northern Canada.

Plant life
In warmer parts of the Arctic lands, ice and snow disappear in summer, and mosses, lichens, grass, small flowering plants and shrubs grow thinly on the stony ground. These are called tundra plants and are the usual kinds of plants found in the Arctic regions. There are no trees, only knee-high shrubs and grasses. In winter the soil freezes solid, and lakes, rivers and streams have a thick covering of ice.

The Arctic region includes both the polar ocean and the northern parts of the continents. The sea ice covering the Arctic ocean is always moving. Each year some of the ice drifts south into the Atlantic and Pacific Oceans. Winds from the Arctic carry cold air into warmer parts of the world. ▶

Canada

Baffin Island

United States of America

◄ People who live in the Arctic are never far from snow and ice. Here, at Qanaq in north-west Greenland, there is ice on the bay and snow on the nearby mountains in summer. In winter the sea will be frozen over and the roads and houses will be under thick snow.

The tree-line

Along its southern edge the tundra merges into the great northern forests of the sub-Arctic zone. This boundary where trees begin is called the tree-line; so the tree-line makes a useful boundary for deciding where the Arctic region extends to on land.

Summer ice

Moving ice floes cover the Arctic Ocean all the year round, though the ice is thinner and melts along parts of the coast in summer. This allows ships to push their way through and travel east and west near the continental coasts.

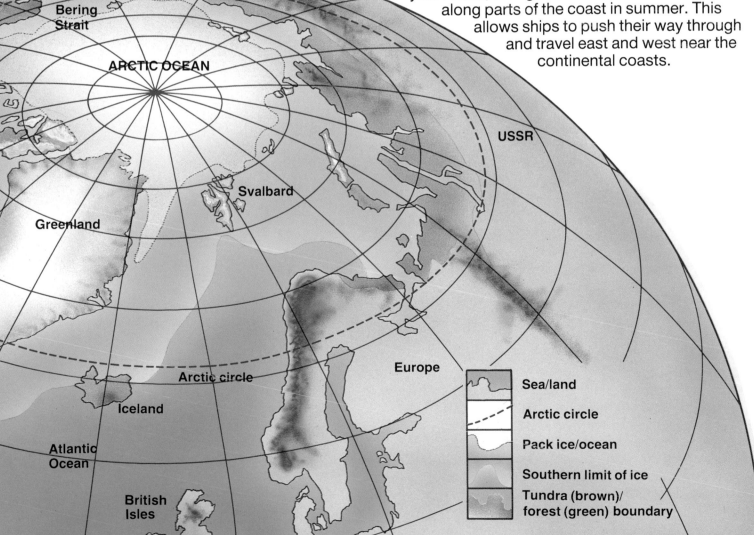

Bering Strait

ARCTIC OCEAN

USSR

Svalbard

Greenland

Europe

Arctic circle

Iceland

Atlantic Ocean

British Isles

	Sea/land
	Arctic circle
	Pack ice/ocean
	Southern limit of ice
	Tundra (brown)/ forest (green) boundary

Around the South Pole

If you are standing at the South Pole, you are high up on an ice cap with 3000 metres of solid ice beneath you. At the Pole itself you will see a line of flag poles with the flags of many nations, and not far away, partly buried under the crunchy snow, lies a permanent US scientific station. The station is called Amundsen-Scott, in honour of the two men who first led expeditions to the South Pole. It is not the coldest or the highest part of the Antarctic, but it is still one of the most difficult parts for people to reach.

Colder and colder

Surrounding you is a featureless plain of snow and ice, with its surface carved by wind into curious ripples and furrows. If you are there in summer the Sun will be shining brightly from an almost cloudless sky; you may feel some of its warmth on your face. The air will be bitingly cold. You will also find it harder to breathe, because air this high up is very thin. In winter it will be dark, though you might see some light from the stars or moon, and a glow from the lights of the scientific station. It will be even colder now, with air temperatures down to −60 °C or lower.

Antarctic travel

Amundsen's party reached the South Pole by dog sledge, and Scott's men trudged all the way hauling their sledges behind them. Both expeditions had to travel for several weeks, and climb dangerous glaciers to get there from the coast. If you go today you will probably fly there in seven or eight hours from the coast, in a comfortable four-engined aircraft. Although the US base is warm and comfortable, you will probably want to leave as soon as you can unless you are a scientist with work to do there. The flight back would take you to land on the sea ice 800 kilometres from the South Pole.

The ice-covered ▶ south polar continent is surrounded by seas which freeze over in winter. Cold surface water spreads from the Antarctic to meet warmer waters from the southern oceans. The boundary where warm and cold waters meet is called the Antarctic Convergence.

The buried land

Almost the whole of the Antarctic continent is ice-covered; less than one twentieth of the land is visible, even in summer when much of the winter snow has disappeared. This ice cap, or the ice-mantle, is formed from snow that has settled over thousands of years, forming into ice under its own weight. The ice has slowly moved downhill to fill the valleys and cover the mountains and plains of the continent beneath. Nobody has ever seen Antarctica free of ice, but we know that the ice is over four kilometres thick in places, and that there are mountain ranges underneath bigger than the European Alps.

There is no tundra in Antarctica, only a very thin scattering of tiny lichens and mosses. They grow in hollows and cracks on north-facing rocky slopes where they can find moisture and a little warmth in summer.

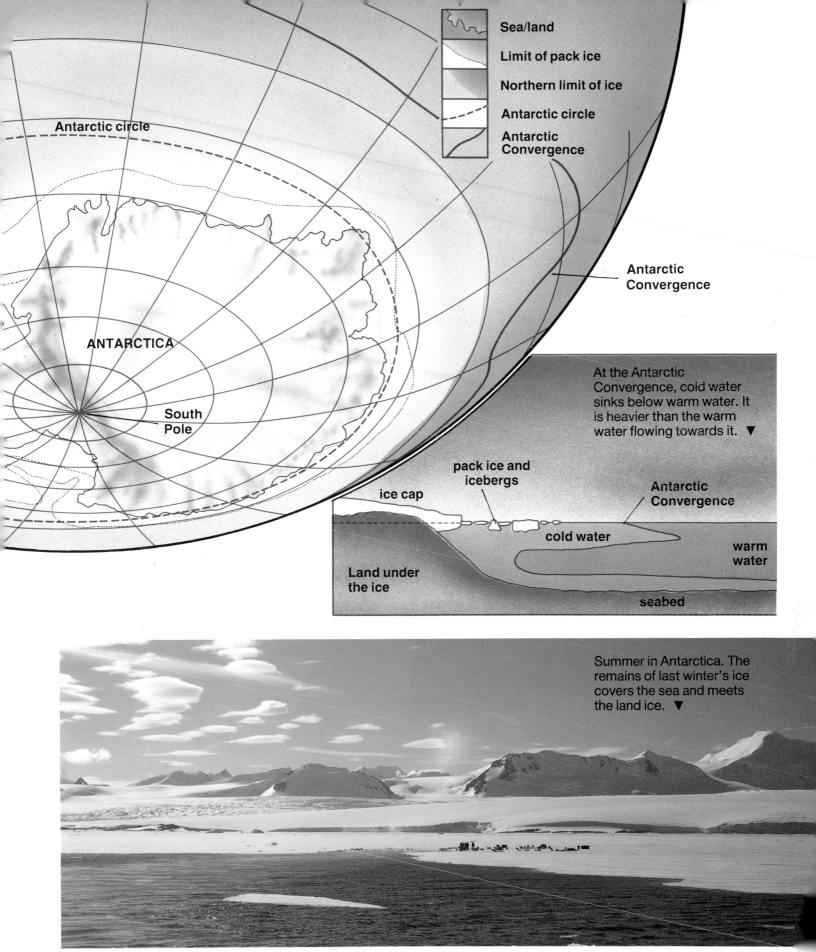

Antarctic circle

ANTARCTICA

South
Pole

Sea/land
Limit of pack ice
Northern limit of ice
Antarctic circle
Antarctic
Convergence

Antarctic
Convergence

At the Antarctic
Convergence, cold water
sinks below warm water. It
is heavier than the warm
water flowing towards it. ▼

pack ice and
icebergs

Antarctic
Convergence

ice cap

cold water

warm
water

Land under
the ice

seabed

Summer in Antarctica. The
remains of last winter's ice
covers the sea and meets
the land ice. ▼

Below freezing

Why are polar regions so very cold? Because the Sun's rays never shine straight down on to them. This means that even in summer the Sun never climbs high in the sky. Though it may shine all day and all night too, it gives very little warmth to the ground or air. Because there is so much white snow and ice, many of the Sun's rays are reflected back into space and never reach the ground to warm it. In winter there is no warming effect from the Sun because it never rises. For these reasons the polar regions do not ever warm up.

The diagram below shows why the Sun never appears above the horizon in winter, and why little warmth reaches the ends of the Earth, even in the polar summer.

The Earth travels around the Sun once a year. In December the Antarctic is tilted to the Sun, and is in sunlight for 24 hours a day. The Arctic is in darkness. ▼

Temperatures

How cold is it at the Poles? At the South Pole, the mean, or average, air temperature for January, the warmest month is −28.6 °C. For the coldest month (July) the mean is −59.7 °C. Temperatures never rise above or even approach freezing point, and constant winds make the cold seem even more severe.

The North Pole is warmer, with summer temperatures close to and occasionally above freezing point, and mean winter temperatures down to about −30 °C. The north polar region is warmer than the south because more of it lies closer to sea level, and the sea helps to keep it relatively less cold.

In June the Arctic is tilted completely towards the Sun, and is in sunlight for 24 hours a day. The Antarctic is in complete darkness. ▼

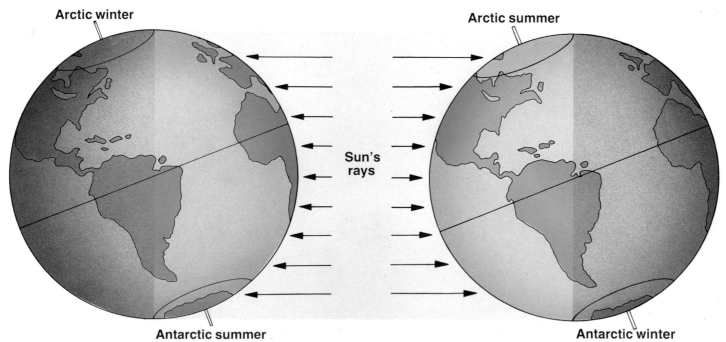

Arctic winter · Antarctic summer · Sun's rays · Arctic summer · Antarctic winter

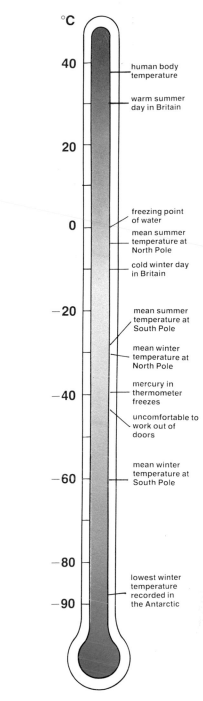

◄ A basinful of water thrown into the air on a very cold day in the Arctic. The water freezes immediately with a loud crackle into thousands of tiny bits of ice.

°C

— 40 human body temperature
— warm summer day in Britain

— 20

— 0 freezing point of water
— mean summer temperature at North Pole
— cold winter day in Britain

— −20 mean summer temperature at South Pole
— mean winter temperature at North Pole
— mercury in thermometer freezes
— −40 uncomfortable to work out of doors
— mean winter temperature at South Pole
— −60
— −80
— lowest winter temperature recorded in the Antarctic
— −90

The coldest areas of the northern hemisphere lie far from the sea and the polar basin, on the high icy plain of Greenland, and in the most northerly parts of Canada and Siberia.

What severe cold does
Strange things happen at very low temperatures. Water freezes and becomes solid, oils thicken to wax, and petrol and paraffin pour slowly. The air is dry, and crackles with electricity. Metals become brittle, and spanners and screwdrivers snap as you use them, and even the mercury in the thermometer freezes.

Danger from the wind
If you are healthy, well fed and well dressed you can work quite comfortably outside at −30 to −40 °C so long as the air is calm. Winds make everything seem much colder, and strong winds whip up the snow into a blizzard. Blizzard conditions can be very uncomfortable and dangerous; you cannot see, and snow gets inside your clothing and melts. At −45 °C your breath steams and freezes in the air; if you breathe quickly, ice forms in your lungs and makes you cough. You have to handle metal objects with gloves on; cold metal can stick to your bare skin and tear it.

How low is the temperature at the back of a household refrigerator, in the freezing compartment, and at the bottom of the deep freeze? How do these compare with polar temperatures?

The lowest temperature you can find in a deep-freeze may still be a lot warmer than a summer day at the South Pole.

(If you are measuring temperatures in a deep-freeze, be very careful, especially if touching any metal). ►

Frozen fingers
Ice collects in your eyebrows and eyelashes. Intense cold may cause you to get frostbite, which can be painful, and severely damage your hands, feet or face. Sunlight reflected from the snow can cause an intense eye irritation, snow blindness, so most travellers wear dark glasses or goggles to protect their eyes.

People working in polar regions must take great care not to be caught out of doors in bad weather. Without warm, dry clothing, food and shelter, they can get into serious trouble very quickly, but with care they can work and travel safely.

Permafrost and tundra

Polar regions are harsh places for plants and animals to live in. The soil is thin and poor. It is usually formed simply from rocks that have been shattered by frost. There is very little humus, or decayed plant material, to enrich the soil or hold moisture. The soil is frozen solid for eight or nine months of the year, and only thaws for a few weeks in summer, so the growing season is short. In summer the ground tends to be waterlogged and marshy, because the soil beneath the surface remains permanently frozen and the melt-water cannot drain away. So tundra vegetation is patchy and thin. Plants are mostly low-lying lichens and mosses, tough grasses and small shrubs. Wild flowers and marsh plants grow in the warmer sheltered areas.

Tiny plants

Tundra plants show many special adaptations. They are mostly small, with wiry stems just a few centimetres long and tiny, tough leaves that can withstand strong winds. Many are dwarf forms of plants familiar to us, dwarf willows, for example that grow less than 30 centimetres tall.

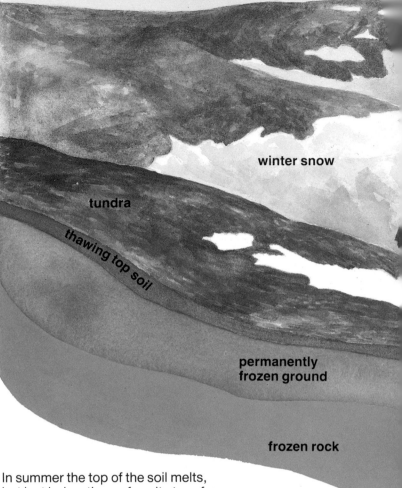

In summer the top of the soil melts, but just below the surface it stays frozen. The soil and rock which stay frozen are called permafrost. The melting of the top layer allows plants a short period of time to grow. ▲

▲ When the surface soil melts each year it is difficult for buildings to stay upright.

Slow growth

Some plants have hairy leaves. The hairs help to protect them from wind. Some grow into 'cushions' up to a metre across, shaped by the wind to cling close to the ground; in the sunshine the cushions warm up, so the plants live at a higher temperature than the air close by. Arctic plants grow slowly. A dwarf willow stem tens of years old may still be no thicker than a pencil. Many of the small shrubs have very wide-spreading roots; there is more of the plant below the ground than above.

For nine or ten months of the year the plants lie covered by a blanket of snow, which shelters them from the sharpest winter winds and hardest frosts. As the sunlight grows stronger in early summer, the snow melts and becomes thin. The thin snow forms a greenhouse over the plants and allows them to start their annual growth before the snow has completely disappeared.

sea

sea ice

seals

reindeer

Insects, animals and humans

Insects are plentiful in summer, including
mosquitoes and small flies that breed in the pools
and emerge to bite warm-blooded animals
(including human beings). Sometimes there are
many mice, lemmings, voles and hares, though
they are often much scarcer after a particularly
hard winter. Ducks, geese and wading birds fly
north from the temperate, warmer regions each
year to rear their nestlings on the tundra. Foxes,
owls and gulls feed on the birds and small
mammals. Musk oxen, reindeer, caribou, moose
and other large mammals graze on the
vegetation, wandering constantly in search of
fresh pastures.

People too can live on the tundra, generally in
small nomadic groups. Some wander with herds
of reindeer. These groups migrate north in
summer, and return south in the winter. Other
groups live close to rivers or the sea.

▲ An Inuit family doing traditional summer
work on the tundra. They are drying meat on
the poles behind them and cleaning the
skins of seals which they have caught out on
the sea ice.

1

LIVING IN THE ARCTIC

Though the Arctic is a harsh place to live, many different kinds of people have spread northward to live there from central Asia, Europe and North America. We know little of the earliest settlers, who first came to the Arctic over 10,000 years ago. Sea level has risen during the past few thousand years and so many of their coastal camp sites are now under water. Some peoples migrated northward or spread east and west when the Arctic was warmer, adapting to increasing cold as the climate slowly changed for the worse. Others are thought to have been driven northward by settlers from the south, and had to find homes wherever they could in a place where few enemies would bother them. All had to adapt to a harsh land where the climate was cruel, food was scarce, and such everyday materials as wood, fuel, workable stone, metals, wool and skins were hard to come by.

Arctic peoples have never been able to develop settled civilizations because they cannot grow crops. With food and shelter so difficult to find, they have generally had to travel for a living. Small groups moved along the coast with the seasons, or migrated between tundra, sea-ice and rivers, to find year-round food. Their few possessions were carried on sledges made of wood, antlers or frozen hides. Their clothes were made from seal, bear or deer skins, cut with stone knives and stitched with bone needles and gut thread; their boats too were made of skin stretched over a framework of bone or driftwood. A few still live this way today, but most have changed their way of life with the coming of 20th century technology.

The edges of this sledge's runners are made of steel. It carries everything an Inuit needs for a hunting trip over the sea-ice to catch seals and fish. Hunters move from one hunting ground to another, and dogs pull the sledges. The paths followed by the hunters are often ones remembered by the old Inuit. ▶

axe and saw
(for cutting ice
and snow)

steel
runners

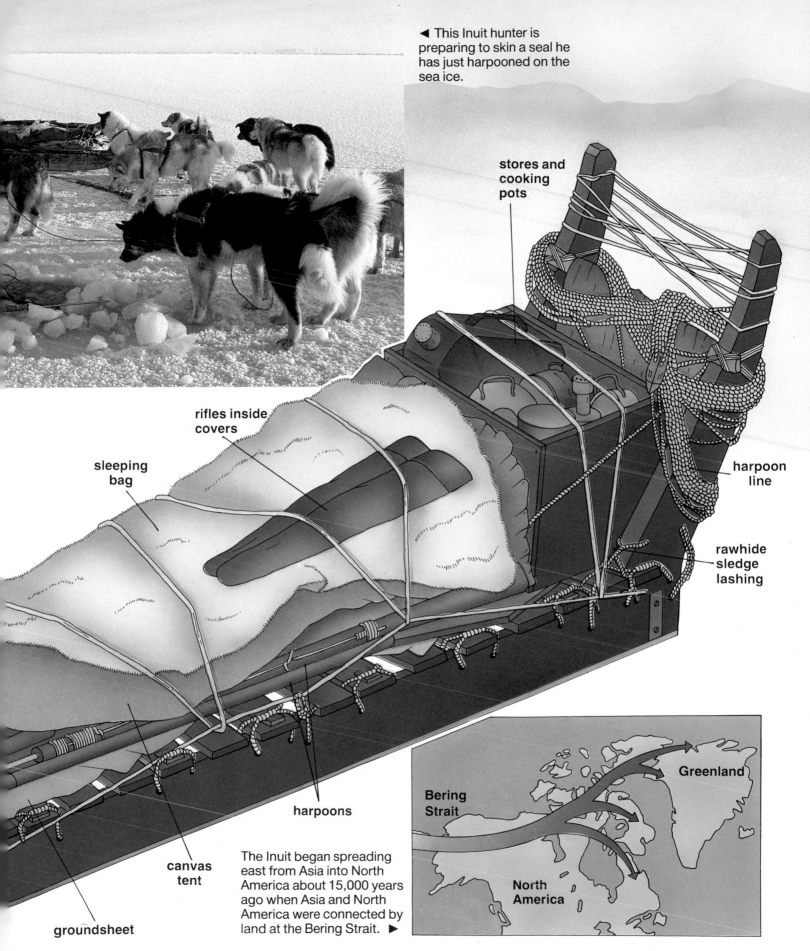

◄ This Inuit hunter is preparing to skin a seal he has just harpooned on the sea ice.

stores and cooking pots

rifles inside covers

sleeping bag

harpoon line

rawhide sledge lashing

harpoons

canvas tent

groundsheet

The Inuit began spreading east from Asia into North America about 15,000 years ago when Asia and North America were connected by land at the Bering Strait. ►

Bering Strait

Greenland

North America

19

Traders and explorers

musk oxen

The Inuit and other northern peoples of Greenland, Asia and North America were isolated by great distance from southern ways of life, and had little contact with them for many centuries. Europeans, for their part, had little reason to visit the harsh, cold lands of the north. The earliest contacts between Europeans and the Inuit took place mainly during the 15th and 16th centuries, when whale and seal hunters sailed northward beyond Iceland and Scandinavia in search of new hunting grounds, and explorers moved north overland through the forests of Asia and Europe to see what lay beyond.

The first contacts were mainly friendly; whalers were glad to meet the local people who could help them with their hunting, and the overland explorers learned useful skills and ways of survival. Before long missions and other posts were established and trade began.

mink

▲ Some of the tundra and forest animals that brought Europeans north to the Arctic. Mink, foxes and otters were hunted for their fur. Musk-oxen were hunted for meat and for their fur by whalers. Walruses provided skins, oil, and ivory tusks. ▶

A meeting in 1819 between Inuit and European seamen, members of a British naval Arctic exploration team. ▼

arctic fox

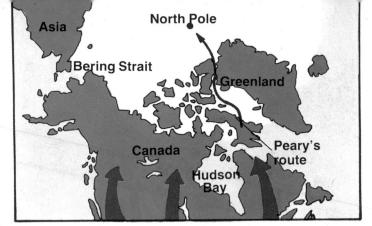

◄ In the 19th century Europeans, Canadians and people from the USA explored the north over land, and naval expeditions explored the sea routes around the Arctic islands. The US explorer Robert Peary reached the North Pole on foot over the sea-ice in 1909.

Exchanging goods

The Europeans took whalebone, whale oil, seal skins, walrus hides, ivory walrus tusks and fish from the northern seas. In the northern forests and tundra they established markets for furs and skins, which they traded for knives, axes, beads and other products from the south.

These exchanges brought many advantages to northern peoples, such as being able to use steel knives for cutting up meat and skins.

wolverine

walrus

New tools

Other gains were steel-tipped harpoons and metal fish-hooks in place of bone, and twine instead of sinews or gut for holding sledges together. But contacts with the Europeans also brought diseases, alcoholism, tobacco and other evils previously unknown in the far north.

Illness and change

Even illnesses like measles and influenza killed many of the Inuit, who had never been exposed to them before. Flour and sugar may have helped some to avoid starvation, but the change in diet made many unhealthy. So most northern communities suffered changes in their ways of life, and many were destroyed altogether soon after the Europeans arrived.

Iceland was discovered by Irish missionaries in the 10th century; Greenland was found by Scandinavian voyagers in the 12th century who settled its southern tip and farmed the land. In the 17th century Danish missionaries and traders made further contacts with Greenland Inuit and colonized the country. The Canadian Arctic and its people were discovered during the mid-19th century when ships of the British Royal Navy sailed north to search for the Northwest Passage.

otter

Summer and winter

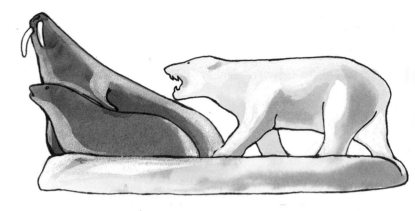

Though the coming of the Europeans changed the lives of many Inuit, there are still a few communities in the far north where families live mainly in traditional style throughout the year. Summer is the busiest time, with the weather at its best and everyone from children to old folks busy every long day. They live mainly in small family groups on the tundra coast or along river banks, in traditional tents of driftwood and skins, in modern tents, or huts made of earth and grass. The men hunt caribou or musk oxen, set snares for Arctic hares and foxes, and traps for polar bears. These provide meat, both for everyday use and to dry over the camp fire for winter. The skins are cleaned, salted and stretched on frames to dry; when ready they can be used for clothing, or for trading with neighbouring groups or down at the store.

Summer fishing

As the rivers thaw the Inuit build dams to catch salmon and char, which at this time of year are swimming upstream in their thousands to the breeding grounds. They catch the fish by hand or in nets, clean and gut them, and hang them up to dry in the Sun. These too can be eaten in winter or traded for store goods.

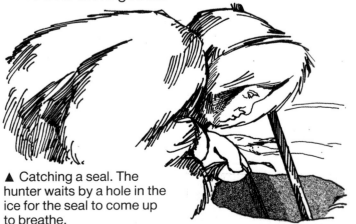

▲ Catching a seal. The hunter waits by a hole in the ice for the seal to come up to breathe.

Sea hunting

As the sea ice breaks up they build and repair their kayaks – flimsy one-man boats of sealskin stretched tightly over a wooden or bone frame. In fine weather they take to the open sea, to search among the ice floes for seals and whales. Harpooned, hauled ashore and cut up, these animals provide meat and blubber.

Many Inuit still make their own clothes from animal furs. They use caribou, seal, or other skins for different kinds of clothing. ▶

22

◄ Figures of walrus, polar bear and people carved by Inuit during the long dark winter months.

Finding food on land

In spring and summer the women with the children hunt for birds' eggs and chicks to eat. They also gather feathers, down, moss and grass for bedding and insulation, and in autumn collect berries for food from the tundra. In summer the women also clean and prepare skins for stitching into clothing or sleeping bags.

Hunting in winter

Winter is a less busy time, though there is still plenty to do during the short hours of daylight. The Inuit often travel over the sea ice with sledges and dog teams to places where they know they can catch seals and fish. They cut holes in the sea ice for fishing; if they are lucky they may harpoon a seal that comes up to use the hole for breathing.

Winter life

During their winter travels the Inuit live in dome-shaped houses built from blocks of tightly packed snow; with oil lamps for heating, these homes can be surprisingly warm and comfortable. With more time for leisure, the Inuit carve in wood, bone and soapstone, sing, play games (cat's cradle is a favourite) and tell each other stories.

In summer earth huts or tents are warm enough for the Inuit to live in. Families like this, who are preparing nets to trap birds, usually go to the same place every year. ▼

Hunters and herders

Every year several kinds of animals migrate to the tundra in summer, and return to the warmth and shelter of the forests in winter. Among these are the caribou of North America and reindeer of Scandinavia, which look very similar to each other and are very closely related. Both males and females have tall, branching antlers. They use these for fighting and for sweeping the snow from their food. They have thick grey-brown fur, especially thick in winter and early spring, and carry a lot of fat that helps to keep them warm.

On the move

Herds of many thousands of caribou and reindeer gather together in early spring to start their northward migration. They follow well-trodden routes, travelling many kilometres every day to reach their traditional northern feeding grounds. Calves are born in late spring. They are able to run alongside their mothers only a few hours after being born, and within weeks can feed on the plants of the tundra. It is a hard life for young animals to survive.

▲ Sami herders of Scandinavia put their reindeer into groups and separate off the young animals. This Sami is lassoing a young male reindeer.

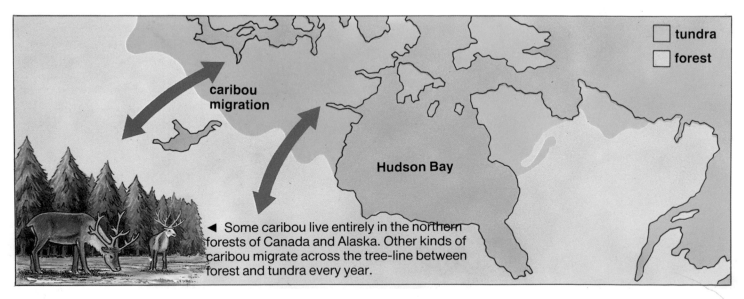

caribou migration

Hudson Bay

tundra

forest

◄ Some caribou live entirely in the northern forests of Canada and Alaska. Other kinds of caribou migrate across the tree-line between forest and tundra every year.

▲ The mountain Chukchi of Siberia are traditionally reindeer herders. This herder is wearing a heavy reindeer-skin anorak.

Wolves and other hunting animals move with the herds, snapping up weaklings. By autumn the calves that survive are sturdy, half-grown animals, ready to join in the long southward march back to the forests.

Building a way of life

In North America, Indians knew where the caribou gathered, and hunted them at different times of the year. The caribou dominated the lives of the tribes that lived along their migration routes. The Indians planned their yearly lives to fit in with the twice-yearly appearance of the animals. In Europe and Asia different relationships were built up between people and reindeer. People in these parts of the world found that they could herd reindeer as well as hunt them. Some tribes moved with the herds. Others kept small domesticated herds for milking, riding and sledge-pulling, while also hunting wild reindeer for meat and skins.

The Sami and the Chukchi

The Sami (Lapps) of northern Scandinavia include both herders and hunters. Mountain Sami travel every year with the reindeer herds which provide them with skins for their tents, clothing, milk, meat and transport. Sami of the forest and coast stay in one place with small domestic herds, and hunt wild reindeer and other animals for their livelihood. Among the Chukchi of Siberia those that lived in the mountains were reindeer herders. Today the Chukchi are mainly settled on farms, though they still keep huge herds of reindeer.

Reindeer in North America

Several attempts have been made to introduce reindeer herding to North America. The first efforts were unsuccessful, for the Indians did not want to give up hunting and turn into herdsmen. Later attempts were more successful, and there are now a few large and profitable herds of reindeer on the Alaskan and Canadian tundra. Reindeer herding creates many jobs locally, and provides skins and meat for sale both locally and in some of the cities further south. There is one small herd of reindeer in Britain, in the Cairngorm mountains of Scotland.

The North now

During the last 40 years, the Arctic has become more important than ever before. It was once the quiet homeland of a few scattered communities, but now it is the centre of much human activity, and many thousands of newcomers have moved there from the south. The shortest air travel routes between Europe and Japan, or between North America and Asia, lie across the icy wastes of the tundra and Arctic Ocean. This means that the Arctic is very important for modern air travel.

But the Arctic is just as important in other ways. Though it is generally too cold for growing crops (except under glass in expensively-heated greenhouses), it has recently been found to be rich in oil, gas, copper, uranium and other useful minerals. These are already being extracted in Alaska, Canada, Scandinavia and Siberia, and small areas of the Arctic are busy with this kind of industrial activity.

This oil drilling station works through the winter darkness at Prudhoe Bay, Alaska. ▼

▲ Deep water ships of the Soviet cargo fleet lining up along a channel cut by icebreakers off northern Siberia.

Wealth in the North

In North America, Arctic oil and gas are particularly important, despite the huge costs of exploration and extraction, and the great distance they have to travel from the Arctic to the southern cities where they will be used. So roads, railways and pipelines have been built across the tundra, and new industrial cities are growing where there was once only tundra or forest. In the Soviet Arctic mineral ores are important, and a great industry has been established to extract them from the Earth, and to refine them.

Arctic technology

The explorers and pioneers of the Arctic today are scientists. They are often geologists and geophysicists who discover likely sites for minerals, often by surveying from aircraft and examining aerial photographs. They visit the sites by helicopter, and send in drillers and riggers who set up test camps to estimate how much oil, gas or mineral ore is present.

Surveyors, engineers and construction-workers bulldoze tracks across the tundra, lay new roads and airstrips, build working camps and refineries, offices, stores, workshops, and permanent housing. Soon the camps become small towns, with their own stores, shops and cinemas.

▲ Some of the oil from wells on the Arctic coast travels across Alaska in this pipeline to Valdez, an ice-free port in the south.

New towns and jobs

Most of the people involved in developing the north are scientists, technicians and skilled workers from the south, many of whom bring their families and make the Arctic their home.

But efforts are also being made to educate and train local people to play their part in development, so that they will benefit from it too. Managers, doctors, nurses, cooks, storekeepers and dozens of supporting workers are needed in the new towns of the north.

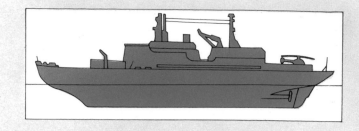

▲ The Soviet icebreaker *Lenin* was the first nuclear-powered ship to enter service at sea, and was launched in 1957.

Arctic Ocean

Ships have been visiting the seas around the Arctic for hundreds of years. Little whaling ships and fishing boats sailed north every summer to the edge of the pack ice, and the wooden ships of the early explorers braved ice and storms to discover what lay beyond. More recently steel trawlers have voyaged far north every summer to the rich fishing grounds off Iceland, Greenland and Alaska.

The pack ice

The most important part of the Arctic Ocean for anyone sailing in it is the pack ice. It is made up of tightly-packed ice floes, some of them many years old. They circulate slowly and even the strongest ships can't sail through them. Around the edge of this old pack lies a ring of newer ice, called annual ice, which forms every winter and breaks up in summer. Most modern ships, though built of steel, are not tough enough to sail through sea ice; even small pieces of ice can pierce the hull of a ship travelling at speed.

Although it sometimes reaches two to three metres thick, this sea ice can be penetrated, but only by specially-built ships called icebreakers. Strongly built, with reinforced steel bows that crush and cut through the sea ice, icebreakers are mostly driven by powerful diesel-electric engines. Some are driven by nuclear reactors which allow them to stay at sea for months at a time without needing to refuel.

Icebreakers, with their thick plates and strengthened, undercut bow, can plough steadily through sea ice over two metres thick, shifting huge floes and even small icebergs out of the way. Where other ships might be crushed by the enormous forces in a big ice-field, icebreakers can withstand them.

sea ice

sea ice

The Arctic pack-ice is home for the polar bear. Scientists examine and weigh a bear which they have caught on land in northern Canada. ▶

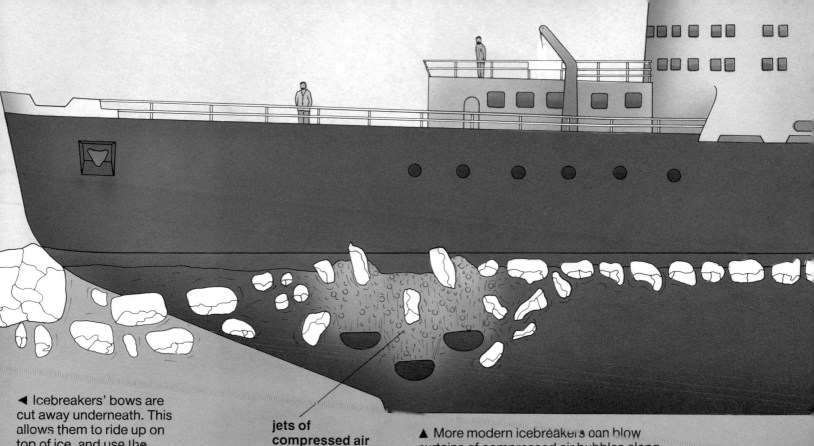

◄ Icebreakers' bows are cut away underneath. This allows them to ride up on top of ice, and use the ship's weight to crush down and break it.

jets of compressed air

▲ More modern icebreakers can blow curtains of compressed air bubbles along the bow. The air bubbles help to move the ice broken by the ship away from the bows towards the stern.

Icebreakers are costly to build and run, but very useful to countries like the USA, Finland, Norway and the Soviet Union, whose ships sail in icy waters. Icebreakers keep the Baltic Sea open to shipping in winter, clear ice from harbours, and allow cargo ships to use Arctic ports for longer every year than would otherwise be possible.

Moving oil from the north

Icebreakers and ships strengthened against ice are used too in the Canadian and Alaskan Arctic. Though there is less need for shipping there at present, the oil and gas which have recently been discovered there cannot be moved out by sea, even in summer, unless there are icebreakers to carve a way through the ice-filled channels. Oil companies are looking for new ways to bring the oil out. Pipelines are a possibility, but are expensive to build and maintain. Submarine tankers that travel under the ice are another possible way. Naval submarines already explore the Arctic sea bed, and tankers that travel underwater might well be important ships of the Arctic future.

Inuit
—modern Eskimos

For hundreds of generations the peoples of the Arctic lived very much in isolation, separated from the rest of the world by empty tundra and forest. First whalers and explorers found them, then missionaries and traders; now teachers, soldiers, doctors, scientists, engineers, builders and social workers have moved into their territory. Not surprisingly, the way of life of almost every northern people has changed, and not all the changes have been for the better.

Having a job
Today many people in the Arctic and sub-Arctic live in villages or small townships, with schools, a store, and possibly a health clinic or hospital. Some adults are employed by the government or the oil and mining companies for building, maintenance, transport, and other jobs that do not need a long training beforehand. Many are in part-time jobs, either because there is no full-time work, or because they like to spend part of their time in the old pursuits of hunting and travelling.

Going to school
Many of the children have regular schooling, though they may have to travel to neighbouring villages or stay some distance from home, to attend secondary schools. A few of the young people who have passed through secondary school may qualify for college training in one of the big settlements or even go to university in one of the big cities. Then they return to their communities as doctors, teachers, lawyers or engineers. Some who see the world outside the Arctic decide not to return to the hard life they left behind, and find jobs in the south instead. But the people of the north are proud of their traditions and cultures, and take care not to be swamped by the ways of life practised by those who live in or come from the South.

Some of the best paid Inuit are the skilled people who can drive heavy equipment on building sites. They do this for some months, and then hunt or fish during other times. ▶

Modern equipment is being used here to reproduce a picture drawn in traditional style by an Inuit artist. Many people like to buy Inuit art. ▼

▲ The check-out counter in a supermarket in the northern Canadian Arctic. There's a lot of choice, but few Inuit have much to spend.

One people

Many now prefer the name 'Inuit' (in their own language meaning 'the people') to the European name 'Eskimo'. Though they belong to three separate nations, the Inuit from Greenland, Alaska and Canada find they have much in common and like to feel that, at least in some ways, they belong to a nation of their own. They learn their own language in school, and many speak it at home.

Keeping traditions alive

Those who are wage earners now buy most of their clothes from the store, but make or buy traditional skin clothing as well for special occasions. Many still know the skills of hunting, fishing and travelling, and teach them to their children. Even though they listen to the radio and watch television and films, they still tell the old stories, sing the traditional songs and enjoy living in the Arctic where they were born.

The future

The 20th century has brought schools, hospitals and wages to the peoples of the Arctic. It has brought machines like skidoos, which some Inuit use to visit their trap-lines and hunt over the sea ice. But the century has also brought drug abuse, diseases, unemployment and other social problems previously unknown in the far north. Should the Inuit have been left to their own way of life, and how much longer will they be able to keep their traditions alive? If you had been born in the Arctic, would you want to stay there?

The route of Cook's voyage around Antarctica. He did not see the continent, but showed where it had to be. ▶

SEARCH FOR THE SOUTH

Antarctica is a long way from the most populated parts of the world. Because of this it remained an unknown continent until the present century. Early Greek geographers thought that a great southern continent must exist, if only to hold the world the right way up. For this reason a south polar land-mass, called Terra Australis Incognito, the unknown southern continent, appeared on old maps, though nobody had actually discovered it. Captain James Cook searched the southern oceans for this unknown continent in the late 18th century. He found and entered the southern pack ice, which is generally thinner than northern pack ice, though still dangerous, and sailed very close to the ice-covered land without seeing it. He judged that the continent would hardly be worth the trouble of finding, even if it did exist.

Antarctica was first actually sighted in the early 19th century. Its discoverers were seamen of Russian and British survey vessels, and sealers from the USA who were hunting for fur seals on the many sub-Antarctic islands of the Southern Ocean. Sealers and British, French and US survey expeditions went on to discover other landfalls in the far Southern Ocean during the late 19th century, sailing their tiny ships into the pack ice in storms and sub-zero temperatures. Whalers were the first to step ashore on Antarctica in 1895. Even then nobody could be sure whether it was a continent, or just another large ice-covered island.

Fur seals like these are now protected against hunting. This group was photographed in the Kerguelen Islands, at the edge of the Southern Ocean. ▶

▲ Nineteenth century sealing ships refined the oil from the seals they hunted.

ANTARCTICA

Cook's route

pack ice

Cook's ships were no bigger than modern tugs, and made of wood. They were very vulnerable to damage in the pack-ice. ▼

Towards the South Pole

It was far from easy to explore Antarctica in the early 20th century, before the days of reliable aircraft, petrol engines and radio. Ships were small and under-powered. They could fight their way only with difficulty across the stormy Southern Ocean and through the pack ice, and then only in the two or three months of summer.

Waiting on the ice

To achieve anything worthwhile it was usually necessary for expeditions to stay over winter, so that they could be ready for an early start in the following spring. On reaching Antarctica they found much of the continental coast hidden under shelf ice or steep glaciers; inland there was nothing but ice and steep mountains, both dangerous to travel on.

All the food, clothing, fuel and equipment they needed for two or three years had to be taken with them, with emergency supplies in case they were shipwrecked or forced to stay longer than they had planned. The climate was bitterly cold, and the winds were very strong, often reaching hurricane force.

Amundsen and Scott started their 1911 polar journeys from the Ross Sea. Shackleton got no closer to the Pole in 1915 than the Weddell Sea. ▶

Shackleton's second expedition (1914–1916) tried to cross Antarctica from the Weddell Sea. His ship *Endurance* was crushed by the pack-ice. ▶

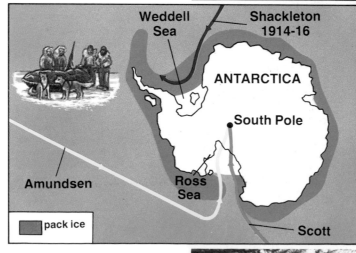

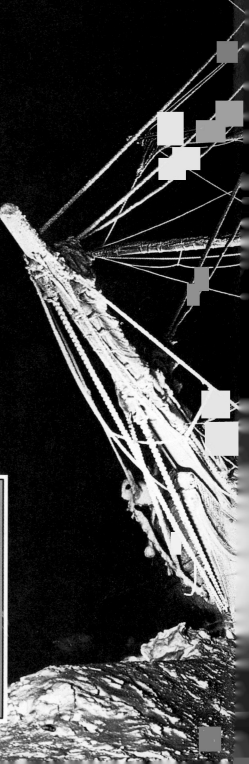

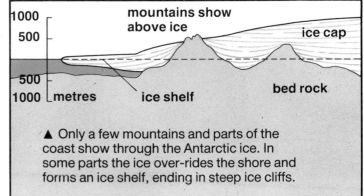

▲ Only a few mountains and parts of the coast show through the Antarctic ice. In some parts the ice over-rides the shore and forms an ice shelf, ending in steep ice cliffs.

Reaching the Pole

Robert Falcon Scott was among the first to explore inland. In 1903 he based an expedition in McMurdo Sound, in the Ross Sea, a piece of coastline that had been discovered by a British naval expedition 60 years before. Scott and his party hauled their own sledges across the glaciers and through the coastal mountains to reach the high polar plateau. One of Scott's companions, Ernest Shackleton, took his own expedition to Antarctica in 1908. He discovered a possible route to the South Pole and nearly succeeded in reaching it. Scott returned with another expedition in 1911, intent on being the first to reach the Pole. However, the Norwegian explorer Roald Amundsen, travelling by a different route and using well-trained dog teams, reached the Pole a few days earlier than the English party. Scott and his four companions died on the long trudge back to their base in McMurdo Sound.

Scientists in the new continent

Belgian, French, US, Australian, Swedish, German and Norwegian expeditions explored different corners of Antarctica before World War 2. They collected rock, plant and animal specimens, made maps, and took surveys. Their work made it clear beyond doubt that Antarctica was a continent, and laid important scientific foundations for later expeditions to build on.

Research in Antarctica started up again during the final years of World War 2, when the first permanent bases were built. By the late 1950s expeditions from over a dozen nations, using icebreakers, aircraft and a network of permanent research stations were co-operating in a huge international effort to solve the continent's remaining mysteries. This effort continues today, with many nations involved.

The Antarctic Ocean

Antarctica is guarded by a ring of deep ocean, narrowest off South America where wild seas separate Cape Horn and the Antarctic Peninsula. West winds blow almost continuously, raising high seas with huge waves between latitudes 40° and 50° south. In the past, sailing ships looking for a fast route to Australia sailed through this ocean. Sailors spoke of the 'roaring forties'. Expedition research ships going to Antarctica today find it just as rough and stormy.

Icebergs

If you are sailing southward in a research ship towards Antarctica, at the Antarctic Convergence, where warm and cold waters meet, (see p. 13), the sea temperature drops several degrees and the air suddenly becomes colder. There are more sea birds in the air, and you may see whales or dolphins in the water. Then the air grows colder still, with squalls of snow or sleet. Small parts of icebergs called bergy bits appear in the water, and larger bergs begin to become visible on the horizon.

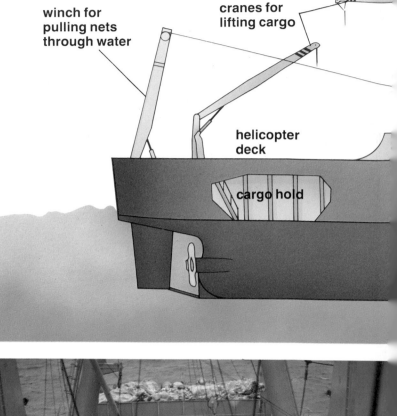

A modern research ship. It has space for cargo, a laboratory, and for comfortable living quarters for the crew. A ship like this can work safely in polar waters when the hull is strengthened against ice. ▶

winch for pulling nets through water

cranes for lifting cargo

helicopter deck

cargo hold

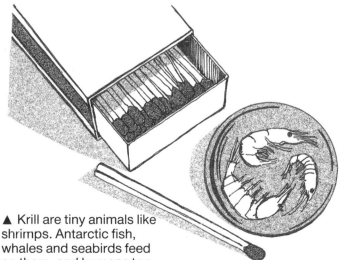

▲ Krill are tiny animals like shrimps. Antarctic fish, whales and seabirds feed on them, and humans too now catch them for food.

▲ The German research ship *Walther Herwig* trawls the Southern Ocean looking for fish suitable to sell in the world's food markets.

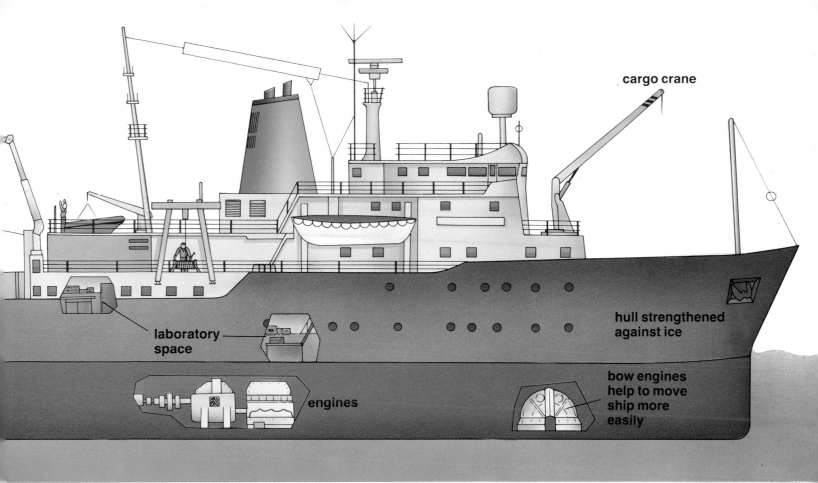

cargo crane

hull strengthened
against ice

laboratory
space

bow engines
help to move
ship more
easily

engines

▲ The RRS *John Biscoe* ploughing south
through the heavy seas found in the 'roaring
forties' to bring food and other supplies to
British Antarctic Survey bases.

The ship keeps well clear of icebergs, for there is
far more ice below the water than above, and
even a glancing blow from an iceberg's huge keel
could tear the hull open. Then the sea turns blue-
green, enriched by microscopic floating plants;
flocks of petrels fly about the ship, and you may
start to see squads of small, darting penguins
swimming alongside.

Approaching the pack ice

A research ship stops from time to time to take
measured samples of sea water from different
depths. It also hauls fine nets that sample the
marine life, and trawls for fish and larger animals.
Heading south again it reaches the first ice floes.
There, it slows to half-speed and enters the calm
world of the pack ice.

At the edge of the pack ice there are broad leads
of blue-green water to sail down between the
floes. Then the ice closes in, and the ship presses
forward through loosely-packed floes, cracking
and pushing them to one side. A research ship
also stops here from time to time for the scientists
on board to sample the water, and to take
readings and measurements.

Exploring a continent

Modern Antarctic research stations are usually made up of a collection of a dozen or more huts. They are placed apart from each other to lessen fire risks, but are linked by covered passageways. The largest bases are usually on the coast and may have accommodation for over 100 scientists and technicians. The walls, floors and roofs of base huts are well insulated by fibreglass against the intense cold. Their windows are double-glazed, and the doors are heavy and tight-fitting like the doors on refrigerators. These help to stop warm air escaping from around the edges of the door-openings. There is always a network of radio-masts, and usually a group of fuel-oil tanks. Generators provide electricity.

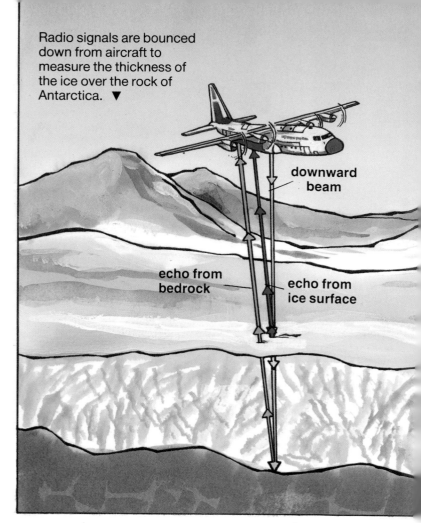

Radio signals are bounced down from aircraft to measure the thickness of the ice over the rock of Antarctica. ▼

downward beam

echo from bedrock

echo from ice surface

A 'Sno-cat' is a warm cabin raised high on four caterpillar tracks. It can carry scientific parties long distances over rough ice and snow. ▶

Cores drilled from the ice give a record of Antarctic snowfall and climate going back many thousands of years into the past. ▼

drill takes samples out of ice

Aircraft with landing skis carry stores to survey parties out on the Antarctic ice. The aircraft are also used for surveying and photography. ▼

What people do on a research station

The biggest stations stand on the coast, because ships can reach them there in summer to bring fresh stores and take people home. Some stations are on stony beaches and free of snow in summer, but deep in snow drifts during the winter. Others in areas of high snowfall are built on ice and may be completely buried in snow with only ventilator shafts and radio masts to show where they are. Inland stations are usually smaller, because they have to be built and re-supplied by aircraft or tractor-train. They too are often built on ice, and sink gradually as the snow builds up over them.

A typical coastal station in summer may have a team of 15 or 20 people operating the base, and 20 or 30 scientists working nearby and in small field parties away from the station. Some expeditions take only men, others include women in their teams. Much of the scientific work will be done by the field parties. They are taken to their sites by tractor sledge or aircraft and left for days or weeks, with food and camping equipment.

Busy summers and lonely winters

There may be two or three visits from icebreakers and re-supply ships during the summer, and stations with airstrips will be constantly busy with the coming and going of cargo aircraft and helicopters. Toward the end of the summer the field parties return to base with their specimens and data. Then everyone whose Antarctic stay is over goes home either by plane or on board ship.

That leaves just a small over-wintering party to maintain the year-round scientific observations. Life is lonely for the scientists who spend the winter in Antarctica, but the stations are comfortable, and there is always plenty to do to keep the winter programme going, and prepare for the next summer's work.

The scientific exploration of Antarctica continues year after year from over 30 wintering stations and many more summer-only stations. Much of the work today is just routine. But some is still new and exciting, and important new discoveries are made every year.

Continent for peace

Antarctica could have been, and could still be, a permanent centre of political trouble. The Antarctic pack-ice was first explored by British seamen; Antarctica itself was first seen by Russians, Americans, and Britons. French, Britons, Americans, Belgians, Norwegians and Swedes were among the first to explore it. Norwegians were the first at the South Pole, and Americans were the first to explore the continent thoroughly by air.

Britain, Australia, New Zealand, France, Chile, Norway and Argentina now lay claim to parts of the continent. Other nations including the USA and USSR do not recognize the claims of the others, and could stake claims of their own if they decided to do so.

The Antarctic Treaty

In fact Antarctica is a continent of peaceful co-operation. Brazil, India, China, Poland and West Germany are among the nations with year-round bases there. Russians and Americans work side by side with Poles, Britons, Japanese, South Africans and people of other nationalities. All are guided by the Antarctic Treaty. Thirteen nations signed this Treaty in 1960–1961, and 19 others have signed it since then. The Treaty says that all these nations agree to work in Antarctica for peaceful purposes only. The question of who owns Antarctica has been put to one side for the moment. Nuclear explosions and the dumping of radioactive wastes are not allowed at all. Information is exchanged freely, and people from different nations work in one another's research stations. There are also frequent international meetings. These ensure scientific co-operation so that each nation knows what the others are planning, and the nations together can achieve far more than by working on their own.

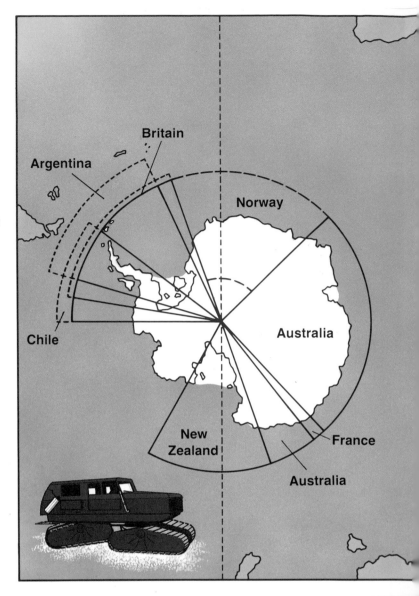

◄ Antarctica is divided like a pie into sections by seven nations with ownership claims. The Argentine, British and Chilean claims overlap. At the moment all nations work together as if no claims existed.

International co-operation

In the past, stocks of seals, whales and fish have been destroyed because no agreements existed about how many seals or whales any nation was allowed to take out of the sea. Now new laws limit fishing in Antarctic waters. A great deal of practical co-operation takes place too. Expeditions help each other no matter what nation they come from and visit each others' stations on friendly terms. Individual scientists and technicians get to know each other personally, exchange ideas and information, and keep each other informed of progress in their work, whatever it may be.

In the 25 years since its beginnings the Antarctic Treaty has proved that nations with very different governments and viewpoints can work closely together and reach agreement on many problems.

Everyone who is a part of the Treaty hopes that international co-operation in Antarctica will help nations to agree, not only in the Antarctic, but in the Arctic and in other parts of the world too.

The modern light-weight sledges being off-loaded from this expedition ship are used by international teams on survey trips. The sledges can carry over half a tonne of stores at a time. ▼

Antarctic scientists meet after their day's work to relax. Months at a time can go by when radio is their only link with the world outside. ▼

Books and Places

Books to read
Exploring Antarctica, Ian Cameron, Longman 1984
Eskimos, Derek Fordham, Macdonald 1979
The Antarctic H.G.R. King, Blandford 1969
The World of the Polar Bear, Thor Larsen, Hamlyn 1978
The Canadian Arctic, S. McCulloch & L. Myers, Longman 1984
Antarctica, S. McCulloch & L. Myers, Longman 1984
Animals of the Arctic, Bernard Stonehouse, Ward Lock 1971
Animals of the Antarctic, Bernard Stonehouse, Peter Lowe 1972
Arctic and Antarctic, D. Sugden, Blackwell 1982

Places to visit
Museums
The British Museum (Natural History) and other scientific museums in London have exhibits of polar plants, animals, geology, fossils and exploration. Aberdeen and Hull museums have displays on Arctic whaling and fishing voyages. The Scott Polar Research Institute museum in Cambridge features exploration of both poles.

Zoos and Oceanaria
Many British zoos keep live polar animals. In Australia visit Sydney's Taronga Park Zoo; in the USA visit Marine World, San Diego.

Expeditions
Every year parties from schools, colleges and activity centres visit northern Norway, Svalbard, Iceland and Arctic Canada. The Exploration Centre at the Royal Geographical Society in London gives advice to people planning expeditions. Arctic travel is expensive, and each person on an expedition should expect to spend the equivalent of several hundred British pounds.

Unfortunately it is more difficult to visit Antarctica, and there are few opportunities, even for young people from New Zealand and Australia.

Events

The North Pole
830–1000 AD Vikings from Scandinavia sailed to Iceland, Greenland and eastern North America.
1576–1615 Martin Frobisher, John Davis, Henry Hudson and William Baffin explored west of Greenland in search of the Northwest Passage.
1594–95 William Barents explored the Northeast Passage and discovered Novaya Zemlya.
1728 Vitus Bering explored the North Pacific Ocean, and sailed through the Bering Strait.
1845–58 John Franklin and successive naval expeditions explored the Canadian Arctic.
1888 Fridtjof Nansen sledged across the Greenland icecap.
1893–96 Nansen drifted in the Arctic Ocean in his ship *Fram*.
1909 Robert Peary sledged to the North Pole.
1926 Nobile, Amundsen and Ellsworth crossed the Arctic Ocean in an airship.
1958 The nuclear submarine USS *Nautilus* reached the North Pole.

◄ Scientist members of Scott's 1910–1912 Antarctic expedition at work in the base hut they built at Cape Evans.

Sending up a weather balloon in the Antarctic. The balloon is filled with a light gas. It lifts a radio transmitter high into the atmosphere, and sends back information about temperature and air pressure. ▶

The South Pole

1497 Vasco da Gama sailed round the Cape of Good Hope.

1772–75 James Cook circumnavigated the Southern Ocean.

1819 Edward Bransfield sighted the Antarctic Peninsula.

1819–21 Thaddeus von Bellingshausen probably sighted the Antarctic mainland.

1837–42 French, British and US expeditions independently charted sections of the Antarctic coastline.

1894–95 First recorded landing on Antarctica.

1899–1900 First expedition to spend a full winter on Antarctica.

1912 Amundsen and Scott reached the South Pole.

1928 Wilkins made the first exploratory aeroplane flights over Antarctica.

1934–35 Ellsworth made the first full flight across the continent.

1944 The first permanent Antarctic scientific bases.

1961 The International Antarctic Treaty came into force.

Word List

Adaptation A particular way in which a plant or animal is suited to its surroundings.

Air temperature The temperature of the air measured by a thermometer shielded from direct sunlight.

Antarctic Convergence The boundary between cold and warmer water at the surface of the Southern Ocean.

Axis An imaginary line through the centre of the Earth around which the Earth rotates.

Blizzard Weather in which snow is picked up from the ground and blown about by strong winds.

Blubber Thick layer of fat found under a whale's or seal's skin.

Caribou A kind of deer found in the North American Arctic region.

Cat's-cradle A game where two or more people make complicated patterns by twining string around their hands.

Celsius degrees A scale of temperature, shown by the sign °C, on which the freezing point of water is 0 and the boiling point of water 100.

Dog-team Group of between five and 13 strong dogs which have been trained to pull a sledge.

Domesticated Describes an animal which has been tamed to live easily with people.

Floe A large flat piece of ice floating on the surface of the sea or a river, usually broken off from a much larger area of ice.

Frostbite The painful result of the skin in the fingers, toes or face becoming frozen.

Geologist A scientist who studies rocks.

Geophysicist A scientist who studies the physics of the Earth and the atmosphere.

Glacier A river of ice flowing slowly downward between mountains.

Harpoon A heavy spear with a sharp metal or stone tip and a rope attached, used in hunting whales, seals and walrus.

Iceberg A large piece of floating ice broken from the ice-mantle.

Ice-mantle A thick layer of ice covering a land area such as Antarctica or Greenland.

Inuit The Eskimo people's own name for themselves.

Kayak An Inuit boat made from skins stretched over a wooden or bone frame.

Landfall The sighting of land after a journey at sea.

Latitude Angular distance on the Earth's surface measured from the Equator. One degree is about 124 kilometres.

Lead A long, narrow opening in sea or river ice.

Lichen Non-flowering, or simple plants that grow on rocks or stony ground.

Mean temperature The average temperature recorded over a period of time.

Melt-water A stream of water flowing from melting snow or ice.

Migration Regular movement of people or animals between one region of the world and another.

Musk ox A large horned grazing animal of the tundra.

Nomadic Wandering from one place to another, usually in search of food or better living conditions.

Oceanaria Places where sea creatures are exhibited.

Pack ice A large area of floes covering the sea or a river.

Permafrost Permanently frozen soil and rock which does not thaw out, even in summer.

Pioneer A person who arrives in a place first, or begins something new.

Skidoo A small motorized sledge which carries a rider and passenger over snow, and can pull other sledges.

Snow blindness A painful eye irritation caused by light reflected from snow or ice.

Soapstone A soft, smooth stone that is easy to carve into shapes.

Sounding Measuring the depth or thickness of water or ice.

Sub-Antarctic The region surrounding the Antarctic.

Sub-Arctic The region surrounding the Arctic.

Traplines Lines of traps set by hunters to catch animals.

Tundra Treeless type of vegetation which grows in polar regions. Also the areas in which it grows.

Index